Managing the Language Classroom

Phil Quirke

English Language Teacher Development Series

Thomas S. C. Farrell, Series Editor

tesol
international
association

Typeset in Janson and Frutiger
by Capitol Communications, LLC, Crofton, Maryland USA
and printed by Gasch Printing, LLC, Odenton, Maryland USA

TESOL Press
TESOL International Association
1925 Ballenger Avenue
Alexandria, Virginia 22314 USA

Senior Manager, Publications: Myrna Jacobs
Cover Design: Tomiko Breland
Copyeditor: Tomiko Breland

TESOL Book Publications Committee
John I. Liontas, Chair
Robyn L. Brinks Lockwood, Co-chair   Guofang Li
Margo DelliCarpini   Gilda Martinez-Alba
Deoksoon Kim   Adrian J. Wurr
Ilka Kostka

Reviewer: Lynn Zimmerman

Copyright © 2014 by TESOL International Association

All rights reserved. Copying or further publication of the contents of this work are not permitted without permission of TESOL International Association, except for limited "fair use" for educational, scholarly, and similar purposes as authorized by U.S. Copyright Law, in which case appropriate notice of the source of the work should be given.

Every effort has been made to contact the copyright holders for permission to reprint borrowed material. We regret any oversights that may have occurred and will rectify them in future printings of this work.

ISBN 9781942223443

Contents

Preface v

1 Introduction 1

2 Develop and Delegate 5

3 Recruit and Respect 15

4 Enhance and Enjoy 20

5 Appraise and Attend 26

6 Mentor and Motivate 32

7 Conclusion: The Students' Voice 37

References 41

About the Author

Dr Phil Quirke is Executive Dean of Education, Higher Colleges of Technology in the UAE. He has been in ELT leadership positions for 15 years and has published on areas as diverse as face, action research, appraisal, and journaling. His book, *An Exploration of Teacher Knowledge*, is widely available, and his publication on reflective writing is available online at www.tesl-ej.org/wordpress/books/.

Acknowledgment

With especial thanks to my current NF22 class, and in particular to Aryam, Maha, Maitha, Mariam Mohamed, Mouza Ibrahim, Noha, Nouf Abdulla, Shamsa Musabah, and Zinab.

Series Editor's Preface

The English Language Teacher Development (ELTD) Series consists of a set of short resource books for English language teachers that are written in a jargon-free and accessible manner for all types of teachers of English (native and nonnative speakers of English, experienced and novice teachers). The ELTD series is designed to offer teachers a theory-to-practice approach to English language teaching, and each book offers a wide variety of practical teaching approaches and methods for the topic at hand. Each book also offers opportunities for teachers to interact with the materials presented. The books can be used in preservice settings or in in-service courses and can also be used by individuals looking for ways to refresh their practice.

Phil Quirke's book *Managing the Language Classroom* explores different approaches to classroom management and the various challenges this may present to a language teacher. Phil provides a comprehensive overview of how to manage language classrooms in an easy-to-follow guide that language teachers will find very practical for their own contexts. Chapters include a general introduction to classroom management with topics on developing the approach to classroom management with the students and delegating responsibilities to students, recruiting to effective classroom teams and respecting everyone in the classroom, enhancing individual skills and enjoying language learning, appraising student learning and attending to the needs of individual students, and mentoring students to build strong learning relationships and motivating students to learn. *Managing the Language Classroom* is a valuable addition to the literature in our profession.

I am very grateful to the authors who contributed to the ELTD Series for sharing their knowledge and expertise with other TESOL professionals because they have done so willingly without any compensation to make these short books affordable to all language teachers throughout the world. It is truly an honor for me to work with each of these authors as they selflessly gave up their valuable time for the advancement of TESOL.

Thomas S. C. Farrell

1

Introduction

This book introduces a fresh approach to classroom management by following the educational management philosophy DREAM, an acrostic formed by the chapter titles:

Develop and Delegate

Recruit and Respect

Enhance and Enjoy

Appraise and Attend

Mentor and Motivate

DREAM covers most areas and issues related to classroom management (Quirke & Allison, 2008, 2010; Quirke, 2006, 2011). The DREAM philosophy places teachers at the core of the institution, and the application of the theory to classroom teaching places students at the core of effective classroom management. Based upon numerous workshops by the author and colleagues, this book gives fresh insights into one of the key pedagogical discussion issues in staffrooms around the world.

What Is Classroom Management?

I like to define classroom management as the ability to create and maintain a conducive, collaborative learning environment with and for students. This is clearly a definition that is simplistic, yet when unpacked it gives us an indication of the true complexity behind our daily work in the classroom—a complexity that is largely tacit in most teachers' knowledge (Wright, 2005, p. 8), and which therefore requires reflection for us to effectively describe what we do in our classrooms (Farrell, 2008).

The "ability to create" emphasises the role of the teacher in setting up the classroom and how the teacher deals with what Wright (2005) calls the "observables" (p. 9) of space, time, learning and teaching activities, communication / interaction, atmosphere, and artefacts.

The "ability to maintain" infers a longer-term commitment to classroom management that requires consideration of Wright's (2005) "unobservables" (p. 16). These include individual affective and cognitive domain factors; group factors; and wider social, cultural, and other influences. The affective domain is reflected most clearly in the participation and engagement of the students that is at the heart of all learning (van Lier, 1996) and effective classroom management (Wright, 2005, p. 17), and is the clearest indication of student motivation.

"Conducive" is a broad term that includes many factors essential to classroom management. Primarily, we must answer the question of "conducive to whom?". And the response must be to our students as a group, addressing Wright's (2005) social psychological factors, and individuals, addressing Wright's affective and cognitive domains.

"Collaborative" addresses the social constructivist (Vygotsky, 1978; Grossman, 1990; Rosen, 1996; Wink & Putney, 2002) nature of language learning, and focuses attention on team building, group formation, and classroom communities (Farrell, 2008).

The "learning environment" is a complex web of interrelationships, which we as teachers can positively shape (Farrell, 2008). "Classrooms are environments where participants through engagement and participation, use and produce resources—social, intellectual and emotional" (Wright, 2005, p. 18).

The inclusion of "with students" in the definition is an indication of the importance of involving students in classroom management, and ensuring students are central in everything we do, consider, and plan for (Fennimore, 2002).

Finally, the term "for students" emphasises the need for the teacher to focus on both individual students and the students as a group when shaping the learning environment for effective classroom management (Farrell, 2008).

The DREAM approach (Quirke & Allison, 2008) to classroom management is a series of 10 principles that ensure students remain at the heart of a structured, practical, and effective method of maintaining student focus that addresses all the factors discussed in the above definition.

Laying the Foundation

Chapter 2 examines the principles of *develop* and *delegate*. The develop principle (Quirke, 2011) focuses on the importance of planning with the students the group's approach to behaviour and interaction: ethos (Scrivener, 2012, p. 232), the aims of the individual students and the group as a whole, and vision (Magy, 2010), an awareness of where they are now in terms of language (mission) and how they will reach their aims (strategy). This chapter emphasises how critical this initial stage is in effective classroom management. The delegate principle reviews how the delegation of teaching roles and classroom activities (Lotan, 2004) can improve classroom management.

Involving Students

Chapter 3 describes the application of the *recruit* and *respect* principles. The recruit principle deals with how we work with students to build effective cooperative learning teams within the class (Ayers & Gray, 2000, p. 5) and how we can use the technological skills of our students to find and develop resources that can support their English language development. Recruit therefore also focuses on building awareness in our students of the infinite number of resources for language learning and practice that surround them even in the most remote contexts. The respect principle explores how teachers can ensure a culture of respect throughout their lessons. This is one of the key features of this approach to classroom management and one that directly addresses those problem classes and undisciplined students often ignored in English language teaching (ELT) literature (Hedge, 2003).

Making Classroom Management Fun

Chapter 4 explores the *enhance* and *enjoy* principles. The enhance principle discusses how a focus on individual student language development plans can dramatically impact classroom management. The enjoy principle emphasizes the importance of humour in effective classroom management (Powell & Andresen, 1985; Smith & Laslett, 1993, p. 38).

Addressing the Individual

Chapter 5 details the approaches taken when applying the principles of *appraise* and *attend*. The appraise principle (Quirke, 2006) focuses on methods to clearly communicate the assessment strategies used to evaluate students' language learning, and the importance of involving students in both the process and assessment from the start of the course. This clarity is essential in any effective classroom management approach. The attend principle refers to how the individual students and their specific needs are addressed in the classroom, and how this requires us to know our students (Underwood, 1987).

Building Strong Interpersonal Student Relationships

Chapter 6 examines the principles of *mentor* and *motivate*. The mentor principle (Quirke & Allison, 2010) reviews how strong interpersonal relationships can be built by using mentoring techniques, which can be applied to the classroom to effectively involve students in peer development (Scott, 2012) and thereby create an environment conducive to learning. The motivate principle then summarises the DREAM approach to classroom management by highlighting the motivational impact each of the other principles has on the students and their language learning.

> ### Reflective Break
>
> - What classroom management issues are you currently facing with your students?
>
> - Which of the 10 DREAM management principles do you expect to help you address these issues?

2

Develop and Delegate

The principle of *develop* concentrates on the first few classes and introducing students to the parameters, rules, and objectives of the classroom and course. It is essential that students feel included and involved in a learner-centred approach (Scrivener, 2012, p. 108–118) throughout the develop stages of classroom management, as this is when the groundwork is laid for all the other principles to be applied successfully.

The *delegate* principle can also be applied from the outset with a new class by handing over the reins to students whenever feasible. The delegate principle should be considered a key part of lesson planning as everything a teacher does as well as how each teacher task can be eventually handed over to students should be explored (Lotan, 2004).

Develop

The first lesson with any new group always sets the tone for the rest of the course and the teaching and learning time together with students. By building the first lesson around students' awareness of their language level (the mission) and involving the students in deciding on the first three or four classroom rules (the developing ethos; Baker & Westrup, 2000, p. 113), you can lay the foundation for a course that runs smoothly with few if any classroom management issues.

The second lesson can include a focus on the learning goals both of the group and the individual students (vision; Murray, 2011, p. 85), development of further classroom rules, and group agreement on the class ethos. This is the moment when, if not already clear, humour and its importance in everything we do can be focused on.

Thereafter, the ethos, mission, and vision can be continuously emphasised as individual language learning plans (see Chapter 4, Enhance) are developed as a strategy for all students to reach their goals. This strategy demonstrates to the students the relevance and importance of the semester, course and lesson plans, and materials, and critically involves them throughout the process as the individual plans are developed.

> ### Reflective Break
>
> - How do you help your students build understanding and awareness of their actual language level in each of the four skills?
>
> - Of the current classroom management issues you identified, how can you turn each one into a classroom rule or Ethos Statement?
>
> - What is your vision for your students?
>
> - What goals do you want them to reach by the end of the course?

The Mission

There are numerous activities that can be used to help students build an awareness of their language level in the four skills (Ur, 1981; Hedge, 1988; Richards, 1990; Nuttall, 1996; Rixon, 1998), and you are encouraged to read the other books in this series for a wealth of ideas (Bleistein, Smith, & Lewis, 2013; Crawford, 2013; Day, 2013; Lessard-Clouston, 2013; Murphy, 2013; Nemtchinova, 2013; Tomas, Kostka, & Mott-Smith, 2013). The following activities have been used successfully with a range of students in a variety of countries at different ages and levels.

Activity 2.1
Reading: Students select a guided reader that they find easy, read the first page, explain it to a peer, and continue through the guided reader levels until they reach a reader that they find difficult to explain.

Activity 2.2
Vocabulary: Students work on a current affairs article selected by the teacher based on the interests of the students. Their only task is to highlight the words that are new to them. They then work in pairs to select the 10 words they think will be most useful to them in this course. The pairs then form a group of four and again whittle the choice down to 10. Then groups of eight narrow the selection to 10 words before the whole class settles on the group of 10 words it thinks are most useful. These words can then be used to have students start their own English language dictionary.

Activity 2.3
Writing: One of the most effective writing activities to raise students' awareness of their ability to communicate meaning is a guided journal launch with students writing about how they use their English outside the classroom. There has been a wealth of literature on journal writing, and readers are encouraged to delve into the power of writing with a focus on fluency, reflective writing, and journaling (Burton & Carroll, 2001; Burton, Quirke, Reichmann, & Peyton, 2009; Farrell, 2012).

Activity 2.4
Listening: There are numerous websites available now for students to explore their listening skills. For example:

    BBC World Service Radio: www.bbc.co.uk/worldserviceradio

    BBC News Video: www.bbc.co.uk/news/video_and_audio/

    ManyThings.Org: www.manythings.org/elllo/

    Randall's ESL Cyber Listening Lab: www.esl-lab.com/

However, some of the most effective awareness building activities are still those using the teacher's voice with students calculating the number of words in a sentence or naming the fourth word in a phrase, for example.

Activity 2.5

Speaking: One of the most effective ways of raising student awareness about their speaking skills and increasing their self-confidence is through audio journals. Students record a brief introduction to themselves at the start of the course and send it to the teacher as an audio file attachment. This allows the teacher to both respond and ask for clarifications.

Activity 2.6

Grammar: Exercises involving both the labeling of texts and the accurate reconstruction of sentences can highlight key weaknesses in students' language, and an alternative can be to turn to the many grammar sites, such as:

> English Grammar Online 4U:
> www.ego4u.com/en/cram-up/grammar

> English Club: www.englishclub.com/grammar/

> British Council Learn English:
> learnenglish.britishcouncil.org/en/english-grammar

There are also many existing grammar activities (Murphy 1992; Eastwood 2006). The teacher can also extract the grammar points to be covered in the course they are beginning to teach and simply ask the students to write example sentences.

Activity 2.7

Integrated Skills: Another effective means of building students' language awareness in the first week of any course is to set a short project in which the students are required to demonstrate their skills in each of the language areas. "A story in the life of my grandfather" is a favourite, as it requires recorded interviews, reading for background details of that era, writing of the story, and a final presentation to the class on their grandfather's life.

Ethos

The first step in any class ethos statement is ensuring that *respect* and *enjoyment* are clearly fronted. Start by modeling the behaviour expected in class and by using humour to address those students who are not respectful, or to simply to cheer up those not enjoying the lesson.

Every teacher has a classroom pet peeve, be it the use of mobile phones or the excessive use of the native language (L1). And every teacher will have his or her own strategy for dealing with these annoyances (Paterson, 2005, p. 37).

Activity 2.8
Restricting mobile phone usage: The teacher can introduce a silent phone rule and, at the beginning of every class, dramatically turn his or her phone to silent and place it face down in the corner of the desk. The teacher then asks all the students to follow suit and introduces this as a classroom rule. Once embedded into the ethos of the class, the teacher could relax the rule by perhaps telling students that if they are expecting an urgent call, they simply have to let the teacher know beforehand and then leave the room quietly to answer the call.

An English-only rule can be implemented and encouraged in a wide array of activities and approaches, and it is a rule that is especially important when teaching a group of monolingual learners. Three activities that have proven successful in the implementation of this rule are the snake (with children), the fine box (with private students), and the sentence completion (with teenagers and young university students).

Activity 2.9
The snake: The snake is a 2-meter long stuffed toy I inherited in my first years of teaching and is simply something no one wants to be left holding throughout a lesson. It could easily be a spider, a red flag, or any other object the students decide is "yucky." The teacher hands the snake to the first student using his or her L1 in the lesson, and it is then the student's task to hand it over to another student as soon as he or she hears an L1. Depending on the level and age of the students, the class and the teacher can decide when the use of the L1 is not beneficial to learning. For example, in beginner level classes, a list of phrases that should be used in English can be drawn up. (E.g., What does that mean?; Can I go to the bathroom?; Please pass me a pen.) When a student uses the L1 for any of these phrases, he or she gets the snake. If done as a game, this simple ongoing activity not only encourages students to use English but can also raise awareness about how useful the L1 is in learning a second language (Gabrys-Barker, 2008, p. 49). It is

important to remember that the focus on the game as fun is absolutely essential and there should be no feeling of punishment. The snake should not stay with any student for a long period of time and should move quickly around the room so there is no sense of having gotten it "wrong," and students listen much more carefully to each other.

Activity 2.10

The fine box: This is another simple way of encouraging students to use English in the classroom. Students agree at the beginning of the course that any use of L1, as agreed upon by everyone in the class, will result in a "fine" of a certain amount. For example, one advanced class I taught in Germany agreed to 1 Deutschmark for every 10 words. Obviously, this is a method that can only work with those who have the money and agree to participate. The usual amount is a matter of pennies per L1 word, and the accumulated pot is then used for an end of course dinner or can even be donated to charity.

Activity 2.11

The sentence completion: This activity is the one of the most successful methods used for encouraging students, and especially teenagers, to use English. A series of dashes is put on the board, representing a mystery sentence that means something to the class. The teacher adds a letter to the sentence for each L1 word used by students during class. For example, this sentence is taken from a recent class after the students had used 20 Arabic words during the lesson: "Phil has never heard so m_ _ _ _ _ _ _ _ _ _ _ _ _ _ _ _ _ _ _ _" (*Phil has never heard so much Arabic in one lesson*). The students not only put peer pressure on each other not to speak the L1 but enjoy trying to guess what the final message will say. Should students use so many L1 words in a lesson that they complete the sentence, a suitable additional task is given to them, such as extra homework. However, if they succeed in not completing the sentence, then the teacher should do a task. This reward of extra work for the teacher always motivates the students, especially if they are allowed to choose the task.

In all these approaches to encouraging the students to use English in the lesson, it is important to move from a strict interpretation of *any* L1 usage to a more relaxed interpretation of L1 usage that is not helping language learning. By drawing attention in this way to the L1 that can support language learning, we can help students appreciate how their native language can be used constructively when learning English (Scrivener, 2012, pp. 214–217).

The Vision

By working with students to draw up a vision for the course and the class as well as for the individual, we can ensure there is a motivational cue that can be fronted on every lesson plan, homework task, or activity.

Activity 2.12

Writing a vision: In one group I am currently teaching, the students require an 80% in their course work to be entered into an early International English Language Testing System (IELTS) sitting as they try and reach the Band 5 they require to start their undergraduate studies. So, our vision, or learning goals, has been shortened to "80%" as there was a collective understanding that every student wanted to maintain 80% throughout the course, and this "80%" became both a motto and mantra among the students. This short numeric vision also allows the teacher to motivate students in a variety of ways, such as keeping their attendance at 80% plus, getting homework completed on time to keep their on-time submission record in our BlackBoard Learn LMS at 80%, and so forth. I have students calculate their ongoing coursework marks and flag their spreadsheet as green (on target), orange (getting there) or red (still loads of work to do). By involving students in the coursework calculations, they start to take greater ownership, and, by being involved, they are increasingly motivated (Stiggins 2001).

Other examples of student visions that have been submitted over the years include:

- "I want to understand my friends' Facebook pages and write nice messages to them that they understand." (9 year old in Caracas)
- "I need to understand the standard business letters I receive and speak to my European clients in a simple, direct and polite way." (German businessman in Bonn)

Some readers may notice the similarity to the A2 Common European Framework of Reference for Languages (CEFR; Council of

Europe, 2013) global descriptor, and this is no accident as these can be used very effectively to help students understand their level of language and the level they wish to attain.

The key to the success of effective student vision statements is ensuring your students understand SMART goals. So, having first asked them to write down what they want to achieve in the course, I ask them the following questions:

- Is your vision specific? Does it say exactly what you want to be able to do?
- Is your vision measureable? Can we understand when you have reached it successfully?
- Is your vision achievable? Can you do this in the time we have on this course?
- Is your vision relevant? Is it about you and your life?

I also add "your vision is time-bound," because the time is set by the length of the course and the time we have together as teacher and students.

I have found this approach a powerful method to help student think about exactly what they want to learn and why it is important for them. I also frame the questions differently depending on the level of the students, but the meaning and focus of each question is the same as the above SMART focus.

> **REFLECTIVE BREAK**
>
> How many teacher tasks could be delegated to students? List as many as you can.

Delegate

From the first lesson, teacher tasks can be delegated to students (Scrivener, 2012, pp. 255–256). The most common tasks delegated by teachers to students are the taking of attendance and board work. By delegating these two teacher tasks to students from the first lesson, a sense of trust and confidence in student abilities can be demonstrated.

This trust and confidence are crucial features in the philosophy of delegation to students, and they are a core principle in the DREAM approach to classroom management. Thereafter, it could be argued that there is no limit to what can be delegated to students.

Ask yourself as you think about your lessons of the past week and look at your lesson plans for the coming week, what could my students do for me? Think about your preparation before the lesson, your teacher role during the lesson, and any correction after the lesson. Teachers can use students to prepare upcoming lessons, and this is a standard approach in many teacher development programmes. While maybe most effective at the intermediate and postintermediate levels, students can be involved in the preparation of lessons at any level as long as the task is level appropriate.

Activity 2.13
Recipe activity: In a lesson on instructions using cooking, recipes, and the vocabulary of food, beginner level students are asked to find anything in their kitchens with English labels. One group in Venezuela came with soup tins, packets of pasta, magazine recipes, a microwave instruction booklet with timings for different food types, and even Sevilla oranges with stickers in English. All the realia was then used to develop student recipes using the language that the students had brought to the lesson.

Activity 2.14
Grammar: More advanced students can prepare grammar presentations to introduce the next lesson. Initially, I work closely with the students so they understand what needs to be covered in such a grammar point introduction, but I have found that students quickly grasp what needs to be done and often address the needs of other students better than I would. When working with lower level students, I would ask them to find examples of the target grammar language point before the next lesson.

Activity 2.15
Reading: For reading lessons, students can bring texts that they want to study and then other students can work on preparing questions from their classmates' texts.

Activity 2.16
Classwork: The technology we work with in the classroom today gives students the opportunity to take over the classroom softboard with their iPad through the Apple TV connection. This gives students great confidence, as they are encouraged to display their work during the lesson and get feedback from their classmates. Students can look for definitions, for example, and the first student to find that definition, picture, or even translation can project it from his or her iPad onto the softboard.

The more complex the task, the more preparation is required, but, ultimately, student involvement in task creation builds trust between students and teacher and builds student self-confidence as they respond to the confidence placed in them by the teacher. These two elements, trust and confidence, are essential in a learning environment that enhances effective classroom management (Loughran & Northfield, 1996, p. 117).

Peer work (Silver, 2008) and correction is another commonly used activity that is also an example of delegation at the initial assessment phase. This booklet will cover assessment in more detail in Chapter 4, Appraise.

Conclusion

This chapter is the longest in the book because the first two principles set the stage for the rest of the DREAM approach to classroom management. Once the ethos of teacher trust and confidence in students has been introduced, the other principles can be applied more effectively.

3

Recruit and Respect

The *recruit* principle deals with how to involve students in building effective collaborative teams and how to use their technical abilities to find and develop good English language learning resources (Savin-Baden & Wilkie, 2006, p. 171) for the benefit of all.

Respect is one of the key features in effective classroom management, and we examine in this chapter how our awareness of the concept of face, the cultural backgrounds of our students (Arabski & Wojtaszek, 2011), and an understanding of how our students perceive respect is essential to good classroom management. We also outline an explicit approach to respect that when discussed with students can help them understand that a raised voice or pointing finger are not the signs of disrespect that they so often take them for.

> REFLECTIVE BREAK
>
> - How do you assign students to groups in your classroom?

Recruit

How can we ensure our students are working in groups and teams that bring out the best in them and their language learning abilities? There are three standard approaches to assigning students to groups when the aim is simply to have students work with each other (as opposed to choosing groups that will most benefit their language learning; Scrivener, 2012, pp. 199–201).

Approach 1

First, simply let students choose who they work with. This usually results in friendship teams, and these can tell the teacher a lot about the class and the collegial relationships forming among the students. (Later, after trying approaches 2 and 3, the group selection can be handed back to the students, who can form their own groups with assigned roles. The teacher can always gain insights from watching a class settle into its new groups and how its reasons for choosing those groups move from friendship to ability.)

Approach 2

Second, the teacher can mix up groups completely randomly by height, month of birth, distance lived from the institute, favourite colour, favourite football team . . . any choice that is not based on learning and which can create totally different groupings each time. The students enjoy the randomness and the language involved in determining what the group will be, and the sense of not being told whom they must work with avoids the all-too-frequent outburst of "I am not working with them." As the students learn to work with everyone else and the teacher continually praises (Kerr & Nelson, 1994, p. 147) individuals for what they give to their current team, the class environment is improved. The teacher can also ask students to assign each other roles such as "researcher," "scribe," "presenter," "timekeeper," and so on.

Approach 3

Third, groups can be assigned based on coursework results to date. For example, in forming groups of four for a writing task, the top writer works with the 5th, 9th, 13th, and 17th in the class writing results. This can be done for any skill and for any number in a group and students appreciate the transparency and rationale behind how the groups are set up.

> ## Reflective Break
>
> - List 15 language resources your students have available to them.
>
> - Then ask your current students to name as many resources as they can.
>
> - Look at the differences and consider this reflection question: What could you do now to better exploit the resources the students have failed to name?
>
> - How can you use the resources that the students named which were not on your list?

The second aspect of *recruit* is the recruitment of resources and the involvement of students in finding good support materials. Whether this is for a specific topic that the class is going to study or a list of good resources for improving English listening skills, for example, the involvement of students in this discovery of resources contributes two factors to effective classroom management. First, it builds on the delegate principle from the previous chapter and, second, it recognizes the technological skills of our students and their ability to find a wide array of online resources and apps to support their language learning.

Activity 3.1
Example 2.5 saw students record a brief 2-minute personal introduction and send it to the teacher by e-mail, having received no instructions about how they should do the recording. The teacher received standard mpeg files attachments, aifc voice messages on iTunes, iMovie recordings, and even cartoon characters with the student's voice.

Activity 3.2
Another activity that works well is to ask students to research resources for a specific skill, such as listening, or an area of language, such as verb tenses, and let the students know that these will be shared around the institute for the benefit of other students—or shared even more widely through a student resource blog or wiki. This approach of "recruiting"

students to find resources builds the trust and confidence begun by the delegate strategies in the previous chapter.

Respect

The most effective way of dealing with respect is to discuss it openly with the students, ideally before any feelings of disrespect manifest themselves through disruption in the classroom. This is because most issues of classroom management begin when either teacher or student is feeling disrespected by the other (Bernstein-Yamashiro & Noam, 2013), and the feeling is then externalised in a range of ways that lead to a loss of teacher control in the classroom. These conflicts can be dealt with by talking openly about respect, and it is even more effective to discuss the issue openly beforehand and show that we as teachers, the power holders in the classroom, do understand the different cultural views of respect that our students hold.

REFLECTIVE BREAK

- What is respect?
- How do you show respect?
- Who do you show respect to?
- When do you feel disrespect?
- Why is respect important?

Activity 3.3
These five Reflective Break questions are the key questions that should be discussed directly with the students, and student responses should be compared to the teacher's answers.

The responses are often fascinating when teaching a monolingual class (Atkinson, 1993) from a culture different from the teacher's, and the awareness raised by comparing responses is truly important to the effectiveness of classroom management. When working with a multilingual, multicultural class (Miller, Kostogriz, & Gearon, 2009), the discussion also helps students understand each other better, which in turn improves the classroom atmosphere and our ability to manage the classroom more effectively.

Activity 3.4

Finally, students can be set the task of giving advice to new teachers arriving in the country for the first time or to a sibling visiting the student's home city for the first time. Students can also be asked to do a presentation, write a brochure, or design a flyer using the same headings as the five questions. After these activities, the teacher should ensure that respect is included in the class ethos statement (DiGiulio, 1995, p. 26).

4

Enhance and Enjoy

The DREAM management principle of *enhance* concerns how teachers can be more transparent with their students and involve them more closely in their language development. (This leads naturally into the Appraise section in the next chapter, where students are involved in the assessment of their linguistic skills; Farrell & Jacobs, 2010, p. 109). This involvement and increased awareness of the way in which language ability develops and is assessed can dramatically impact the effectiveness of classroom management.

The principle of *enjoy* is crucial in learning, as it lowers the affective filter (Krashen, 1982). This section brings the use of humour and its importance to the fore in language learning, student motivation, and classroom management (DiGiulio, 1995, p. 58).

Enhance

Enhance builds upon the principle of delegate (Chapter 3) and toward the principle of appraise (Chapter 5). It focuses on how students can be encouraged to take more responsibility for their learning both inside and outside the classroom (DiGiulio, 1995, p. 17). The more involved students are in the development of their language learning, the easier it becomes to manage the classroom as students perceive the importance of and the need to be in the classroom. Individual language development plans are one effective tool in accomplishing this, and we can draw upon numerous ways to assess our students' language learning styles to help in creating these development plans (see Reid, 1998; Dunn & Griggs, 2000; Scrivener, 2012, pp. 100–106).

Activity 4.1

VARK (which stands for four types of learning styles: visual, auditory, read-write, and kinesthetic), is a type of assessment frequently seen in ELT classrooms; students find it easy to understand, and there are many resources available online. Every learner will apply a combination of learning styles. Online questionnaires, for example those available through the VARK website (http://www.vark-learn.com/english/index.asp), help teachers to understand which style predominates in a particular student and which style students learn best with.

By doing these questionnaires, students raise their awareness of their learning styles. In addition, the teacher's lesson planning can be better informed. Once completed, teachers can explicitly demonstrate to students that their lessons are aimed at the learning styles of the students, and students can better understand why teachers use a variety of activities and presentation techniques.

Activity 4.2

The VARK results can also be used to set homework tasks that are targeted to the specific learning styles of the students. For example, when preparing for a lesson using a text on the Dubai Expo 2020, the students who are visual are asked to find and view a video on the Dubai Expo bid, the auditory are asked to call the Dubai Expo information line in English, the read-write are asked to find recent news clippings on the bid, and the kinesthetic are asked to go to the information centre and find information or realia that can be used in the class.

These learning style–targeted tasks outside the classroom begin to build an understanding in the students that they need to take responsibility for their learning, and this can then be emphasised by encouraging students to work on all their language skills in their own time. Once again, there is a wealth of ideas for teachers to use, and I encourage readers to refer to the other books in this series (Bleistein, Smith, & Lewis, 2013; Crawford, 2013; Day, 2013; Lessard-Clouston, 2013; Murphy, 2013; Nemtchinova, 2013; Tomas, Kostka, & Mott-Smith, 2013). A few examples of self-directed learning tasks that have been used successfully would include:

Activity 4.3
Weekend reading: Students choose what they want to read and submit a weekly report that is simply one sentence on what the book is and how many pages they have read, and a second sentence stating what they have enjoyed reading (or not enjoyed reading). The focus is on the reading and the enjoyment of reading rather than on the writing of a summary or a description.

Activity 4.4
Journal writing: Students write whatever they want and decide if they want to share their writing and with whom. All the teacher needs to see is that something has been written. If students choose to share their writing with the teacher, the teacher should respond to the content but not correct the language. The teacher will explain to the students that the focus is on fluency and not accuracy, which tends to be the focus of most classroom writing.

Activity 4.5
Listening to news: Students are asked to listen to English news channels on TV, radio, and the Internet in preparation for a weekly (or daily) discussion on current world affairs.

Activity 4.6
Speaking: Students are encouraged to do any of the above or any homework task as a recording and submit it for the teacher to respond to.

Individual Plan
All the above activities also work well as classroom coursework. Such coursework, along with test results, allows the teacher to prepare an individual student language development plan that highlights areas each student can focus on. These plans are short and focused, and change during the course. As students learn to understand their language levels, needs, and goals better, they eventually suggest their own additions to their plans and take more control. Figure 1 is an example from a student aiming to get a Band 5 IELTS so he can enter the university's degree programme.

	Student Name
Reading	*Read the story of the UAE founder and write 10 quiz questions to ask the class next week.* *http://www.uae-embassy.org/uae/history/sheikh-zayed*
Writing	*Tell me what you have done over the past weekend and remember to check your tenses*
Vocabulary	*Look at the HCT B1 Word list. Select 10 new words that you want to use in your writing this week.* *https://www.vocabulary.com/lists/187039#view=list*
Grammar	*Review the past simple versus past continuous by doing these exercises: http://www.esl-lounge.com/student/grammar /2g50-past-simple-or-past-continuous-worksheet.php*
Listening	*Try one of the Medium Listening Quizzes for Academic Purposes from http://www.esl-lab.com and let me know if you found it easy or difficult*
Speaking	*Record yourself saying any tongue twister you like from http://www.twisterking.com/p.php*
Pronunciation	*/p/ - /b/: look at the chapter from Ship or Sheep*

Figure 1. Language Development Plan

> **REFLECTIVE BREAK**
>
> If you were asked to draw up an individual language development plan for one of your students, what would you include?

These individual language development plans (Figure 1) do not take long to put together, especially once the students become involved in suggesting ways they can work on their language and start taking responsibility for their learning.

Enjoy

E is the central letter of DREAM, and *enjoy* is the central theme of the DREAM approach to classroom management. This principle emphasises the belief that happy students create the environment that is most conducive for effective learning and classroom management. Essentially, we enjoy teaching, we enjoy teaching our students, and we continually demonstrate this to them.

This, of course, presupposes that we do indeed enjoy teaching our students, no matter how difficult they may be. All teachers have had those classes where every student seems to be aiming at making the teacher's life as impossible as he or she can. The most effective response to such classes is humour (Gokhale, 2006) and the ability to show the teacher can take whatever is thrown at him or her, turning the negative into a positive. The teacher's perseverance will eventually win over the most belligerent and difficult class, but we must keep our sense of humour by being true to ourselves (Scrivener 2012, pp. 36–39). It also means understanding the students' humour and responding to it while maintaining the principle of respect that all have agreed upon.

There are several ways that the principle of enjoy can be explicitly worked on with students. When a class is flat or the atmosphere is worse than that, teachers should take a break from the lesson plan and create an enjoy stage in the lesson.

> ### REFLECTIVE BREAK
>
> What would you include in a 10-minute enjoy stage?

Activity 4.7
Students can simply be asked what makes them happy, how they show that they are enjoying a lesson, or what the biggest laugh they had recently was.

Activity 4.8

Higher-level students can be asked to tell a favourite joke, and lower level students can view a humourous clip—from Mr. Bean, for example (see www.mrbean.com/clips).

Activity 4.9

Writing captions to cartoons is another enjoy activity that works well. These interjected enjoy stages (DiGiulio, 1995, p. 58) often alleviate the atmosphere and demonstrate to the students that the teacher is not fixated on covering what has to be covered, but that he or she is also aware of their feelings and the mood of the class.

Activity 4.10

Another effective strategy is to tell personal stories (Morgan & Rinvolucri, 1988), especially those that are strange, different, and amusing. These short anecdotes allow the students to see the teacher in a different light instead of purely as an authoritarian figure. This does not mean getting too personal with the students or relinquishing the teacher role, but it does mean treating your students as individuals whom you are interested in (Smith & Laslett, 1993, pp. 10–11). Teachers cannot expect students to trust them and contribute unless teachers also trust the students and talk *to* them rather than *at* them. Each teacher will find the approach, humour, and level of appropriateness that works for them, but to ignore the personal will always have a negative impact on the effectiveness of our classroom management.

5

Appraise and Attend

Appraise focuses on not only how teachers communicate assessment strategies to the students but also how students can be fully involved in the evaluation of their language skills and those of their peers and classmates (Farrell & Jacobs, 2010). *Attend* is all about how students should be addressed as individuals (Jonson, 2008, p. 63) and how teachers can attend to the specific needs and language development of their students both in the classroom and beyond.

Appraise

Involving students in the whole process of their assessment in a course is one of the key principles in the DREAM approach to classroom management, and it builds upon the strategies of delegate and enhance outlined in previous chapters. It can be stated with some confidence that most classroom management issues begin from a student's sense of disempowerment and lack of understanding of how they can possibly succeed in a particular course. By involving them explicitly in the assessment process, we address this issue before it arises.

There is a wealth of literature on assessment practices (See O'Malley & Pierce, 1996; Hughes, 2003; McNamara & Roever, 2006), not least the book *Language Classroom Assessment* in this series (Cheng, 2013), and readers are encouraged to explore every method of assessment available to them, especially those that are more formative. The key to the DREAM approach to classroom management is openness and transparency with the students. This means having a full plan of the assessment for a particular course prepared in advance and showing this to the class from day one. It means explaining to students clearly how each element of the assessment is calculated and exactly what they need to do to get a particular mark. It means demonstrating to them how their work is marked and involving them in peer assessment and self-assessment (Ambrose, Bridges, DiPietro, Lovett, & Norman, 2010, p. 225) whenever possible. This transparency builds students' confidence and their language awareness. In this way, assessment becomes a tool in the linguistic development of our students and not an evaluative, summative, or punitive measure.

> **REFLECTIVE BREAK**
>
> How can you involve your students in the assessments you currently use?

Most courses today use some form of learning management system, which includes a database for coursework calculation (e.g., Blackboard Learn, Banner, Moodle), and these can be creatively adapted to include peer assessment and transparency for students to calculate their ongoing coursework marks and grades.

By including in your classroom the following activities, which involve students in peer correction, you are able to explore all your assessments and how you can involve your students more in the process.

Activity 5.1
Student conferencing: When teachers take the lead at the start of the course in student conferences (Katz, 1996, p. 72) and, using individual student language development plans to support the discussion, guide students to ways they can improve, students move toward taking a greater lead and suggesting ways they can improve their own coursework.

Activity 5.2
Speaking: When students give assessed presentations, the teacher can give their classmate audience the same assessment sheet that he or she uses. The first time, the teacher can do a mock presentation for the

class; all students and the teacher complete an assessment. The class then discusses the results, and the teacher explains his or her assessment marks. Finally, the student markers who give the closest marks to the teacher's can be awarded a bonus. The student assessments can then be counted toward the overall presentation grade. Peer assessments should be worth anywhere from 20 and 50% at the beginning stages, and as students become more proficient in their marking, the peer assessment percentage can be raised, and self-assessment can also be introduced. This works particularly well when using the band descriptors for CFR, IELTS, FCE (First Certificate in English), or other common international assessment instruments as the descriptors help raise students' linguistic awareness and their understanding of how their own work is marked.

Activity 5.3

Writing: When marking students' written work, it is often effective to first give individual students a focus and a bonus for the features they find. For example, after a student writing task, students can assess each other's writing in groups with each student taking a different focus: one on past tenses, one on capitalization and punctuation, one on spelling, and one on understanding meaning. Each student is asked to highlight errors and give prompts, using, for example, a standard correction code (e.g., *svagr* for subject-verb agreement). Then, the students can be given a chance to write a second draft before the teacher marks both drafts, awarding bonuses for the accuracy of student marking as well as the final essay.

Activity 5.4

Vocabulary: Students mark each other's vocabulary tests and only those words all students answer correctly are removed from the vocabulary test list. The test becomes a group effort to reduce the list to be learned and a group assessment mark could be awarded every month. This group assessment method works well for linguistic items that are most effectively learned in a rote manner (e.g., irregular past tense forms) as the group applies both peer pressure and classmate support.

Having students regularly review their coursework standing and giving them opportunities to address work that can be improved are other features of this approach to assessment.

Activity 5.5

Homework: One of the most effective methods I have found in ensuring students complete homework assignments is to ask them to work in small groups (up to four students) but then submit by e-mail their part of the assignment individually. I then collate the four submissions into one document (or presentation, or slideshow, etc.) and respond to all four together for collective correction. If I respond to each submission quickly, copying in the other members of the group on the e-mail, I have found that students are motivated not just to complete their submission quickly but also to work collectively on their corrections.

Summary

This approach to appraisal is a key feature of the DREAM approach to classroom management. It addresses both overall coursework and individual assessments in a transparent manner that helps students understand exactly how they attain the marks they are awarded. It builds both students' awareness and confidence, and as their confidence and empowerment over their learning increases, so does the effectiveness of our classroom management.

> **REFLECTIVE BREAK**
>
> - Did you find any appraisal/assessment methods in this section that you have not used before?
> - How effective would this approach to assessment be with your current students?

Attend

If we see *appraise* as a quantitative approach to classroom management issues, then *attend* is the qualitative, humanistic approach. This principle depends on the teacher knowing their students as individuals, caring about them as individuals, and demonstrating this continuously. We attend to the details, which affect the day-to-day learning of our students, and never ask any student to do a task that we would not do ourselves. This latter point is an important one.

Activity 5.5
If the teacher does the same task as the students, it both motivates them and gives them a model to assess their work against. I first discovered the power of this approach when writing journals (Burton & Carroll, 2001) with my students, but it works equally well with any writing task, material discovery, grammar example searches, reading comprehension exercises done in class, or listening homework tasks from the web. By doing the work, the teacher demonstrates to the students that the task is important for the course and they can draw upon the teacher's model as well. It also minimizes how often teachers hear students use the "lack of time" excuse for not doing their homework—if the teacher can complete the same task with his or her workload, students certainly should have the time.

Activity 5.6
The other key element of attend is the teacher knowing his or her students and demonstrating this knowing to them. This can best be demonstrated by setting tasks and activities that are relevant and personalized to the students (Nunan, 1989).

To do this, teachers need to know their students as individuals. Many of the standard introductory first-week activities can be used to start this process (Scrivener, 2012, pp. 82–87). Activities or ice breakers such as "find someone who . . . ," "have you ever . . . ," "my favourite holiday," and "my family stories" can all help teachers build a picture of each student.

The teacher can continually demonstrate to the students that he or she heard their input and is getting to know them. This can be done throughout each lesson by using teacher asides and humour, and in the comments made on work that is marked. The individual language development plans are also a key feature of demonstrating how well a teacher knows his or her students.

> **REFLECTIVE BREAK**
>
> How do you demonstrate to your students that you know them as individuals?

Summary

When teachers demonstrate that they know their students, attend to their language learning needs as individuals, and appraise them fairly and transparently, while showing the students that they enjoy teaching them, then the foundation for effective classroom management has been laid.

6

Mentor and Motivate

Mentor reviews how mentoring techniques (Malderez & Bodsczky, 1999) can be applied to the classroom in order to effectively involve students in peer development and thereby create a more conducive language-learning environment. *Motivate* reviews the impact that the DREAM approach can have on classroom management by highlighting the motivational impact each of the DREAM management principles has on students and their language learning.

Mentor

Mentoring can be simply defined as a process by which one person helps another in order to achieve something (Jonson, 2008). It is a way to help and support in a manner that the recipient appreciates, and it empowers the recipient to move forward with confidence toward achieving his or her desired goals (see Figure 2). Mentoring is also concerned with creating an informal environment in which one person can feel encouraged to discuss his or her needs and circumstances openly and in confidence with another person who is in a position to be a positive help (Jonson, 2008). Mentoring is about creating a safe environment and enabling students to ask questions. While all the above is true of the teacher, this section examines how teachers can give students the confidence to mentor other students.

The mentor can be a student who has a stronger language level in a specific skill than the mentee. It can be a student who has been at the institute longer than the mentee, and/or who has better learning skills. In all these cases, we can help students form a mentor relationship that boosts the mentor's confidence while helping the mentee with the skill or institutional knowledge he or she lacks.

Activity 6.1

The easiest mentoring relationships to set up are those at the beginning of any new course or year, when students who have attended the school, college, or institute before can be "buddied" (Graf, 2011, p. 61) with new students so that the latter can be guided around the intricacies of any new establishment. The mentor student should be given a guide that lists the support he or she promises to give to the new student. An example of one such guide is shown in Figure 2.

Activity 6.2

The mentoring experience can be moved into the classroom, for example, by pairing strong writing students with weaker writers to work on drafting essays, and by introducing peer assessment (Ecclestone, 2010). In order for this mentoring approach to work, the reason for pairing the students together must be explicitly stated. One way of doing this is using the coursework grading sheets and demonstrating how the students with the top marks are paired with those who have the lowest marks to date. By pairing students according to the language skill or the task being worked on, students do not feel discriminated against.

I promise that I will

    Provide orientation to the college facilities

    Advise on college procedures and practices

    Be open-minded

    Clarify essential issues

    Maintain confidentiality

    Be accessible

    Encourage the new student to participate in college activities

    Give encouragement

    Give emotional and moral support

Figure 2. Example of a Student Mentor Guide

Weaker students should also be encouraged to mentor younger or lower level students outside the classroom, for example, during library reading hours. This can also give these students confidence and show them that they, too, have a lot to give.

The confidence that students gain from mentoring other students and the learning-based interrelationships formed among students during the process enhance the effectiveness of our classroom management.

> ### Reflective Break
>
> How could you use these mentoring partnerships with your students?

Motivate

The most important element in motivating students is involving them in every aspect of their learning, the classroom, and the day-to-day life of the institution, while listening to them and understanding their needs and the motivational factors that drive them. Maslow's (1970) seminal work on motivation lists five levels of motivation related to the following needs:

1. Biological and physiological—air, food, drink, shelter, warmth
2. Safety—protection from elements, security, order, limits, stability
3. Belongingness and love—work, family, affection, relationships
4. Esteem—self-esteem, achievement, mastery, independence, status, dominance, prestige, responsibility
5. Self-actualization—realizing personal potential, self-fulfillment, seeking personal growth, and peak experiences

Translated into the DREAM model through the label of *motivate*, the highest level (5) is self-actualization, or the need for self-fulfillment (Trotzer, 2006, p. 71): a sense that one's potential has been fully realized. It is suggested that this is a stage that one needs to work on continuously throughout a lifetime, and teachers must therefore continually address this need through daily praise and demonstration that they appreciate student work.

The fourth level in Maslow's (1970) hierarchy refers to the need to develop self-esteem through personal achievement (Mruk, 2006, p. 78), as well as social esteem through the recognition and respect we get from others (McBride, 2013, p. 51). Therefore, teachers must support students in the setting of attainable goals (vision) and publicly recognise their attainment of these goals.

Maslow's (1970) third need is the sense of belonging that refers to an individual's need for love, affection, and interaction with other people. By focusing on a class ethos of enjoyment as the central tenet of the DREAM philosophy, teachers can ensure that students have a strong sense of belonging.

The lower two elements of Maslow's (1970) hierarchy are safety and physiological, and they involve the need for a secure and stable environment with basic biological needs such as food, clean air and water, and adequate shelter. These basic biological needs should be satisfied outside of the institution, but the classroom should provide a secure and stable environment (Grossman, 2004, p. 139) no matter what the chaos outside might be. Teachers must always demonstrate to their students that they are concerned for their students' basic welfare and be responsive to any concerns that students voice.

Teachers motivate their students by following the other principles closely. Motivate is the DREAM principle that links all the other principles together:

The motivation of inclusion—Develop

The motivation of belonging—Recruit

The motivation of personal advancement—Enhance

The motivation of purpose—Appraise

The motivation of responsibility—Delegate

The motivation of Respect—Respect

The motivation of happiness—Enjoy

The motivation of recognition—Attend

The motivation of collaboration—Mentor

REFLECTIVE BREAK

- Which element of motivation in this section is most relevant to your current teaching situation? Why?

- How will you introduce the motivational strategies from the relevant DREAM principle to your classes?

By following all the DREAM principles outlined in this book, teachers can ensure their students are well motivated and thereby increase the effectiveness of their classroom management.

7

Conclusion: The Students' Voice

The previous section on *motivate* summarised the impact the DREAM approach to classroom management has on students from the perspective of the author and teachers. This conclusion draws upon feedback from students and their experiences with the DREAM approach to classroom management.

Develop

The classroom management strategies that my students have found most useful under *develop* include using English-only in class, developing the class ethos (and especially the silent mobile phone agreement), the vision of sitting IELTS early with an 80% coursework achievement, the weekend readings, the weekly reference to the coursework spreadsheet, the development of personal dictionaries to study vocabulary, and journals.

Delegate

Under *delegate* the strategies highlighted by the students were the ability to choose the subject for their presentations on culture, the ability to choose the books they wanted for the weekend reading, the open correction technique employed for first drafts (which does not use a correction code but simply highlights where a mistake has been made), the opportunity for students to take over the classroom softboard with their iPad through the Apple TV technology, the ability to choose the groups they work in and finish early once their tasks have been completed.

Recruit

The strategy which most impacted the students under *recruit* was giving them the freedom to choose their teams, the team leaders, the class representative that would be their voice on the college Student Council, and the group leaders who submitted the work on distance classes when the teacher was not in front of the classroom.

Respect

The students were very particular that the most important aspect of the *respect* principle was the respect they felt they were given by the teacher. They felt they were given respect by the way the teacher talked to them politely and listened to them, hearing their opinions and understanding their excuses. They also mentioned the importance of the teacher smiling and repeating instructions when not understood.

Most interestingly, all students who gave their input also stressed that they show respect to the their fellow students by emulating their teacher's example and adhering to the class ethos.

Enhance

The students focused on the following teacher strategies for *enhance*: support us to take the IELTS sooner; help us to improve our English by giving us the new vocabulary we need, have us write journals, encourage us to read regularly on the weekend, help us to work together, teach us differently, improve our self-confidence and personality, make us speak English only in class, help us increase our marks by understanding the work we must do.

Enjoy

Students wrote more under the *enjoy* principle than any other, and they all stressed the use of humour in the lesson and their confidence in the fact that they knew their teacher enjoyed teaching them, because "he was happy and respect us." Several other students also linked their enjoyment to the respect they felt for and from the teacher and added that they wanted to return that respect by completing the work set, following instructions, speaking English, and paying attention in class.

The students also stated that their sense of enjoyment was enhanced because they felt confident and comfortable in sharing their ideas and interacting with one another. The final teacher characteristics that students said were important to their enjoyment of a course were fairness and kindness. Students stated they would respond to both of these by working cheerfully without complaint and smiling every day.

Appraise

The teacher's classroom management strategies under *appraise* that were most appreciated by the students were fairness, rapid response to e-mail submissions, clear indication of errors, the requirement to make corrections to earn coursework marks, and the focus on drafts and process writing.

Attend

The key feature of teacher behaviour for students under *attend* was the ability to listen to what the students said and care about what they were saying. Students pointed out that they appreciated the teacher looking at them when they spoke and responding in ways that showed he had listened to what they had said. Interestingly, students said that they were happy to attend the classes when they felt a teacher listened to them. The teacher's interest motivated them to attend classes and participate constructively.

Mentor

Student responses to the mentor principle demonstrated that they considered *mentor* much more than one-on-one support for each other. Mentor, for these students, refers to how they support each other and build good study teams within the classroom. Several students stressed features of the class ethos and DREAM management as essential for good mentor relationships and constructive teamwork. These included everyone working hard for each other, dividing tasks among the team, cooperating with each other, listening to each other, respecting everyone in the group, openly discussing solutions, knowing one another, and having confidence in each member to do his or her work.

Conclusion: The Students' Voice

Motivate

Students stated that the teacher strategies that they found most motivating included support (Scrivener, 2012, p. 120), the English-only rule, the variety and number of different activities, the weekly review of grades and guidance in the work needed to raise those grades, and constant praise and encouragement. Above all, the students appreciated the push to be the best they could be.

Conclusion

The students' responses support the belief that the DREAM approach to classroom management is effective. The approach is not revolutionary and does not introduce any specifically new strategies, but it does pull numerous teacher techniques into one consistent approach to classroom management which, when applied from the first lesson, does result in a well managed classroom with motivated students willing to work with each other and for the teacher.

References

Ambrose, S. A., Bridges, M. W., DiPietro, M., Lovett, M. C., & Norman, M. K. (2010). *How learning works: 7 research-based principles for smart teaching.* San Francisco, CA: Jossey-Bass.

Arabski, J., & Wojtaszek, A. (2011). *Aspects of culture in second language acquisition and foreign language learning.* Berlin, Germany: Springer-Verlag.

Atkinson, D. (1993). *Teaching monolingual classes.* Harlow, England: Pearson Education/Longman.

Ayers, H., & Gray, F. (2000). *Classroom management.* London, United Kingdom: David Fulton.

Baker, J., & Westrup, H. (2000). *English language teacher's handbook: How to teach large classes with few resources.* London, England: Bloomsbury.

Bernstein-Yamashiro, B., & Noam, G. G. (Eds.). (2013). *Teacher-student relationships: Toward personalized education: New directions for youth development, number 137.* Hoboken, NJ: Jossey-Bass.

Bleistein, T., Smith, M. K., & Lewis, M. (2013). *Teaching speaking.* Alexandria, VA: TESOL International Association.

Burton, J., & Carroll, M. (Eds.). (2001). *Journal writing.* Alexandria, VA: TESOL International Association.

Burton, J., Quirke, P., Reichmann, C., & Peyton, J. K. (2009). *Reflective writing—A way to lifelong teacher learning.* Retrieved from http://www.tesl-ej.org/wordpress/books/

Cheng, L. (2013). *Language classroom assessment.* Alexandria, VA: TESOL International Association.

Council of Europe (2013). *Common European framework of reference for languages: Learning, teaching, assessment.* Cambridge, United Kingdom: Cambridge University Press. Retrieved from www.coe.int/lang-CEFR

Crawford, W. J. (2013). *Teaching grammar.* Alexandria, VA: TESOL International Association.

Day, R. R. (2013). *Teaching reading.* Alexandria, VA: TESOL International Association.

DiGiulio, R. (1995). *Positive classroom management.* Thousand Oaks, CA: Corwin Press.

Dunn, S. R., & Griggs, S. A. (2000). *Practical approaches to using learning styles in higher education.* Westport, CT: Greenwood.

Eastwood, J. (2006). *Oxford practice grammar*. Oxford, England: Oxford University Press.

Ecclestone, K. (2010). *Transforming formative assessment in lifelong learning.* Maidenhead, United Kingdom: McGraw-Hill.

Farrell, T. S. C. (2008). *Classroom management.* Alexandria, VA: TESOL International Association.

Farrell, T. S. C. (2012). *Reflective writing for language teachers.* Sheffield, London: Equinox.

Farrell, T. S. C., & Jacobs, G. M. (2010). *Essentials for successful English language teaching.* London, England: Continuum International.

Fennimore, B. S. (2002). *Student-centred classroom management.* Albany, NY: Delmar Publishers.

Gabrys-Barker, D. (2008). *Morphosyntactic issues in second language acquisition.* Bristol, United Kingdom: Multilingual Matters.

Gokhale, S. B. (2006). Get the best out of every average student. In V. Kirpal (Ed.), *Secrets of good teaching* (pp. 49–57). Hyderabad, India: The ICFAI University Press.

Graf, M. (2011). *Including and supporting learners of English as an additional language.* London, England: Continuum International Publishing.

Grossman, P. (1990). *The making of a teacher: Teacher knowledge and teacher education.* New York, NY: Teachers College Press.

Grossman, H. (2004). *Classroom behavior management for diverse and inclusive schools.* Lanham, MD: Rowman & Littlefield.

Hedge, T. (1988). *Writing.* Oxford, England: Oxford University Press.

Hedge, T. (2003). *Teaching & learning in the language classroom.* Oxford, England: Oxford University Press.

Hughes, A. (2003). *Testing for language teachers*. Cambridge, United Kingdom: Cambridge University Press.

Jonson, K. F. (2008). *Being an effective mentor: How to help beginning teachers succeed*. Thousand Oaks, CA: Corwin Press.

Katz, A. (1996). Teaching style: A way to understand instruction in language classrooms. In K. M. Bailey & D. Nunan (Eds.), *Voices from the language classroom* (pp. 57–87). Cambridge, United Kingdom: Cambridge University Press.

Kerr, M. M., & Nelson, C. M. (1994). *Strategies for managing behavior problems in the classroom*. New York, NY: MacMillan.

Krashen, S. (1982). *Principles and practice in second language acquisition*. Oxford, England: Pergamon Press.

Lessard-Clouston, M. (2013). *Teaching vocabulary*. Alexandria, VA: TESOL International Association.

Lotan, R. A. (2004). Stepping into groupwork. In E. G. Cohen, C. M. Brody, & M. Sapon-Shevin (Eds.), *Teaching cooperative learning: The challenge for teacher education* (pp. 167–182). Albany, NY: State University of New York Press.

Loughran, J., & Northfield, J. (1996). *Opening the classroom door: Teacher, researcher, learner*. London, England: Routledge.

Magy, R. (2010). *Learner goal setting*. Harlow, England: Pearson Longman. Retrieved from http://www.pearsonlongman.com/ae/emac/newsletters/RMagy_Monograph.pdf

Malderez, A., & Bodsczky, C. (1999). *Mentor courses: A resource book for teacher trainers*. Cambridge, United Kingdom: Cambridge University Press.

Maslow, A. H. (1970). *Motivation and personality*. New York, NY: Harper & Row.

McBride, C. (2013). *Recognition*. Cambridge, United Kingdom: Polity Press.

McNamara, T., & Roever, C. (2006). *Language testing: The social dimension*. Oxford, England: Blackwell.

Miller, J., Kostogriz, A., & Gearon, M. (Eds.). (2009). *Culturally and linguistically diverse classrooms: New dilemmas for teachers*. Bristol, United Kingdom: Multilingual Matters.

Morgan, J., & Rinvolucri, M. (1988). *Once upon a time: Using stories in the language classroom*. Cambridge, United Kingdom: Cambridge University Press.

Mruk, C. (2006). *Self-esteem research, theory, and practice: Toward a positive psychology of self-esteem*. New York, NY: Springer.

Murphy, J. (2013). *Teaching pronunciation*. Alexandria, VA: TESOL International Association.

Murphy, R. (1992). *English grammar in use*. Cambridge, United Kingdom: Cambridge University Press.

Murray, G. (2011). Imagination, metacognition and the L2 self in a self-access learning environment. In G. Murray, X. Gao, & T. Lamb (Eds.), *Identity, motivation & autonomy in language learning* (pp. 75–90). Bristol, United Kingdom: Multilingual Matters.

Nemtchinova, E. (2013). *Teaching listening*. Alexandria, VA: TESOL International Association.

Nunan, D. (1989). *Designing tasks for the communicative classroom*. Cambridge, United Kingdom: Cambridge University Press.

Nuttall, C. (1996). *Teaching reading skills in a foreign language*. Oxford, England: Heinemann.

O'Malley, J. M., & Pierce, L. V. (1996). *Authentic assessment for English language learners: Practical approaches for teachers*. Boston, MA: Addison Wesley.

Paterson, K. (2005). *55 teaching dilemmas: Ten powerful solutions to almost any classroom challenge*. Ontario, Canada: Pembroke Publishers.

Powell, J. P., & Andresen, L. W. (1985). Humour and teaching in higher education. *Studies in Higher Education, 10*(1), 79–90.

Quirke, P. (2006). A coherent approach to faculty appraisal. In C. Coombe (Ed.), *Evaluating teaching effectiveness in EFL/ESL contexts* (pp. 89–105). Ann Arbor, MI: University of Michigan Press.

Quirke, P. (2011). Developing the foundation for DREAM management. In C. Coombe, L. Stephenson, & S. Abu-Rmaileh (Eds.), *Leadership and management in English language teaching* (pp. 67–79). Dubai, United Arab Emirates: TESOL Arabia.

Quirke, P., & Allison, S. (2008). DREAM management: Involving & motivating teachers. In C. Coombe (Ed.), *Leadership in English language teaching & learning* (pp. 186–202). Ann Arbor, MI: University of Michigan Press.

Quirke, P., & Allison, S. (2010). Building leaders through mentoring. In J. A. Carmona (Ed.), *Language teaching and learning in ESL education: Current issues, collaborations and practice. Leadership skills for English language educators*. Matthews, NC: Kona Publishing.

Reid, J. M. (1998). *Understanding learning styles in the second language classroom.* Upper Saddle River, NJ: Prentice Hall Regents.

Richards, J. C. (1990). *The language teaching matrix.* Cambridge, United Kingdom: Cambridge University Press.

Rixon, S. (1998). *Developing listening skills.* Oxford, United Kingdom: Macmillan.

Rosen, H. (1996). Meaning-making narratives: Foundations for constructivist and social constructionist psychotherapies. In H. Rosen & K. T. Kuehlwein (Eds.), *Constructing realities: Meaning-making perspectives for psychotherapists* (pp. 3–49). San Francisco, CA: Jossey-Bass.

Savin-Baden, M., & Wilkie, K. (2006). *Problem-based learning online.* Maidenhead, United Kingdom: McGraw-Hill.

Scott, K. (2012). *Enhancing student support: Peer support report.* Edinburgh, Scotland: EUSA.

Scrivener, J. (2012). *Classroom management techniques.* Cambridge, United Kingdom: Cambridge University Press.

Silver, R. E. (2008). Monitoring or observing? Managing classroom peerwork. In T. S. C. Farrell (Ed.), *Classroom management* (pp. 45–55). Alexandria, VA: TESOL International Association.

Smith, C. J., & Laslett, R. (1993). *Effective classroom management.* London, England: Routledge.

Stiggins, R. J. (2001). *Student-involved classroom assessment.* Upper Saddle River, NJ: Merrill Prentice Hall.

Tomaš, Z., Kostka, I., & Mott-Smith, J. A. (2013). *Teaching writing.* Alexandria, VA: TESOL International Association.

Trotzer, J. (2006). *The counselor and the group: Integrating theory training and practice.* New York, NY: Routledge.

Underwood, M. (1987). *Effective class management.* New York, NY: Longman.

Ur, P. (1981). *Discussions that work.* Cambridge, United Kingdom: Cambridge University Press.

van Lier, L. (1996). *Interaction in the language curriculum: Awareness, autonomy and authenticity.* London, England: Longman.

Vygotsky, L. S. (1978). *Mind in society.* Cambridge, MA: MIT Press.

Wink, J., & Putney, L. (2002). *A vision of Vygotsky.* Boston, MA: Allyn & Bacon.

Wright, T. (2005). *Classroom management in language education.* Basingstoke, United Kingdom: Palgrave MacMillan.

The English Language Teacher Development Series

Reflective Teaching (Thomas S. C. Farrell)
Teaching Reading (Richard R. Day)
Teaching Listening (Ekaterina Nemtchinova)
Teaching Vocabulary (Michael Lessard-Clouston)
Teaching Speaking (Tasha Bleistein, Melissa K. Smith, and Marilyn Lewis)
Teaching Grammar (William J. Crawford)
Cooperative Learning and Teaching (George M. Jacobs and Harumi Kimura)
Teaching English as an International Language
(Ali Fuad Selvi and Bedrettin Yazan)
English Language Teachers as Program Administrators (Dan J. Tannacito)
Classroom Research for Language Teachers (Tim Stewart)
Teaching Writing (Zuzana Tomaš, Ilka Kostka, and Jennifer A. Mott-Smith)
Teaching Pronunciation (John Murphy)
Content-Based Instruction (Margo DelliCarpini and Orlando B. Alonso)
Language Classroom Assessment (Liying Cheng)
Teaching Digital Literacies (Joel Bloch and Mark J. Wilkinson)
Teaching English for Academic Purposes
(Ilka Kostka and Susan Olmstead-Wang)
Lesson Planning (Nikki Ashcraft)
Motivation in the Language Classroom (Willy A. Renandya)
Classroom Interaction for Language Teachers (Steve Walsh)
Managing the Language Classroom (Phil Quirke)

Coming Soon:
Teaching Young Learners (Helen Emery and Sarah Rich)
Materials Development (Steve Mann and Fiona Copland)
Language Teacher Professional Development (Thomas S.C. Farrell)

tesol
international association

www.tesol.org/bookstore